DOING THE FAITH

DOING THE FAITH

by
T. Leo Brannon

Designed and illustrated by
Harold Bales

tidings
1908 Grand Avenue
Nashville, Tennessee 37203

Library of Congress Card Catalog Number: 7295654
E006B.

TO

Bishop W. Kenneth Goodson, my spiritual mentor, who gave me a chance to glimpse a beautiful blending of vital piety and administrative skill, and whose trust allowed me to reach for maturity in understanding and action.

CONTENTS

PREFACE

This study of James has not only provided me new insights, it has led me in new paths. Through this study I have been strengthened in new ways of personal ministry.

My debt to many others is beyond repay. My friend, Walter Albritton, Jr., has been "an encourager" ever since we trudged uphill to seminary classes. Working on a student newspaper together during seminary days first taught us how to work together. I hope this effort demonstrates we still know the art of cooperative endeavor.

My family shared in this effort through their understanding love for a negligent father and husband. My wife, Martha, has freed me to work when she had every right to expect me to be with the family. Scott and Susan, young as they are, have displayed unusual patience with a father who was preoccupied.

During the time of this manuscript's preparation my mother had a stroke and was recovering. Those hours spent in writing should have been spent in letters of encouragement to her. I am sure she wondered why no word from me as weeks passed with no letter. Perhaps she will understand that it wasn't total negligence.

Ashland Place Church has provided a splendid setting for this endeavor. They have joined me in this venture with real enthusiasm. Our able church secretary, Mrs. W. C. Gray, has given invaluable assistance in deciphering scribbled notes and typing the manuscript.

There are many others who have aided this endeavor but space and time prevent a complete listing. Suffice it to say I am in debt to many and especially to friends who share their lives with me.

Set some goals you want to achieve in this study. What do you hope to learn? What help do you want to gain? What questions do you need answered and ideas clarified?

The author of this book is designated simply as James. This could have been either one of three such men by this name in the New Testament: James, the son of Zebedee, James the less, and James, the Lord's brother.

Most Bible scholars favor James, the Lord's brother, as the writer. He appears in Mark 6:3 as one of the four brothers of Jesus. In Acts 12:17 his position in Jerusalem is suggested and in Acts 15 his authority in the Council of the elders is noted. No doubt his family relationship with Jesus gave him status in the early church. Yet, there seems to be more than this to account for his strong position of leadership.

Who wrote the book is not crucially important. We know that the writer was quite familiar with the teachings of Jesus which had been handed down in oral form. There are many similarities to the Sermon on the Mount and other portions of the Synoptic Gospels.

James is the English translation of the Hebrew and Greek "Jacob." The name Jacob suggests the father of the twelve tribes of Israel. Probably the author or editor selected this name to suggest that now the church as the New Israel has a new leader in James of Jerusalem.

The letter was addressed to the "twelve tribes scattered abroad." By this is meant all Christians everywhere who need moral instruction and guidance in the new faith.

Circle words you do not understand. Look them up in a dictionary. Discuss them with others.

The letter is not one of profound theology. It is a letter of practical instruction regarding the practice of the Christian life. The writer has collected traditional instructions to be circulated among the churches to use in their training of disciples or believers.

A practical faith must be rational, reasonable, relevant.

Purpose of the book was to provide concrete ethical instruction for the readers during the moral crisis of that day. In our own time we are faced with a moral crisis of no small proportion. The book of James can be of great benefit to us as we answer some basic moral questions.

What is the nature of our present moral crisis?

In this study/action guide we will deal with the highlights of the letter and seek to relate them to the situation today. Where we fail to make the instructions to apply to our lives today, we urge the readers to search out the application.

Simply put, the letter of James seeks to answer for his readers the question: "What does a Christian *do* about his faith?" Our aim in this study is to help you to find your answer to this question. It is

What does a Christian do about his faith?

Get together resource material from your church library and other sources which you will use in this study.

not enough to exult in the experience of God's grace; we must relate it to real life. To be sure, it is far easier to remain within the inner realms of personal experience. But, the gospel is not divided into the inner and outer; it is a whole and demands to be treated as such.

In our day there is sharp division between the generations over the matter of hypocrisy. Accusation and counter-accusation leave us with broken communication and damaged relationships. At the least it demands extra effort to make sure our practice of the faith is consistent and true.

Too many with an "establishment" orientation are confusing twentieth-century, middle-class mores with the morals and values of the gospel. There is a distinct difference. This younger generation is asking that we recognize the difference and then "put our money where our mouth is." We are challenged to risk all for the gospel and leave the neat security of middle-class values to those whose hope is only in this age.

With the rise of the "Jesus Movement," lay witness movement, and other evidences of spiritual hunger, many people feel we are on the verge of a new revival of religion. Whether this occurs or not, we need to train those who are committed to Christ in the practice of the faith. There are a great many people in our church fellowship who have never learned to put into practice their faith.

For many it would make a vital experience of faith if they discovered an active practice of personal ministry. Too many of our people are imprisoned in a small world of passive ideas about faith. Liberation occurs when you discover that you are called to a ministry of setting men free, feeding them, giving sight to blind men, and otherwise being involved in an active personal ministry.

Those who witness to the gospel need to discover that it means more than just talk. Our witness has to be done in deed as well as word. It is not enough to say I have discovered God's love for me; it is imperative to demonstrate it by showing love to others and in deeds of mercy.

This is precisely what we hope to discover in this study. While the book does not pretend to be a scholarly commentary, it has sought to help you find the answer to the question of how to practice the life of faith. However, I hope it evidences responsible study of the works of Bible scholars.

Listen to the recording from which the title of this chapter is taken. Think of the scripture verses this song sounds like.

chapter 1

I Never Promised You A Rose Garden

Life is not always easy and pleasant. Like the song says, "into every life some rain must fall." Problems are a part of life. Jesus cautioned his disciples, "in the world you will have tribulation." We are not promised a "rose garden" or easy road to travel.

The writer of James urges his readers to meet the trials and troubles of life with a positive attitude. He suggests that there are underlying values in the tribulations and temptations that they will face. Rather than let adversities defeat them, they rejoice because such trials strengthen their faith and lead to a full, meaningful life.

Roger Hazelton reminds us that even Christians are not immune to the difficulties of life. He writes, "A Christian's life is just as precarious and vulnerable to destructive power as any other sort of life. We live as much at the brink of disaster and are equally prey to the claims of despair. There is to be sure, a genuine security and

(1:2-4; 12-18)
Count it all joy, my brethren, when you meet various trials, for you know that the testing of your faith produces steadfastness. And let steadfastness have its full effect, that you may be perfect and complete, lacking in nothing.
Blessed is the man who endures trial, for when he has stood the test he will receive the crown of life which God has promised to those who love him. Let no one say when he is tempted, "I am tempted by God"; for God cannot be tempted with evil and he himself tempts no one; but each person is tempted when he is lured and enticed by his own desire. Then desire when it has conceived gives birth to sin; and sin when it is full-grown brings forth death. Do not be deceived, my beloved brethren. Every good

endowment and every perfect gift is from above, coming down from the Father of lights with whom there is no variation or shadow due to change. Of his own will he brought us forth by the word of truth that we should be a kind of first fruits of his creatures.

(2 Cor. 12:7-9) And to keep me from being too elated by the abundance of revelations, a thorn was given me in the flesh, a messenger of Satan, to harass me, to keep me from being too elated. Three times I besought the Lord about this, that it should leave me; but he said to me, "My grace is sufficient for you, for my power is made perfect in weakness." I will all the more gladly boast of my weaknesses, that the power of Christ may rest upon me.

serenity which faith in God brings; but it ought not to be confused with a magic island of refuge, a privileged immunity, or a pair of seven league boots for overstepping the boundaries with which all human life is hedged."[1]

We discover our weakness and strength through testing. Paul points out that strength is to be found in a consciousness of personal weakness. (2 Cor. 12:7-9) By no means are we to take a defeatist attitude. Yet, without an understanding of where we are weak and where we are strong, we are unable to build up our lives.

James says that the value of trials and troubles is that they enable a person to endure. This seems to be a prevalent attitude in the New Testament. Paul reminded the Christians in Rome: "Let us exult in our present sufferings, because we know that our suffering trains us to endure, and endurance brings proof that we have stood the test" (Romans 5:3-4).

Endurance is what makes a champion. He keeps on going, sometimes after all the indications are that he is licked. He just won't quit. The Duke of Wellington, in comparing the French and the British soldiers, said, "The British soldiers are not braver than the

[1] *God's Way With Man* by Roger Hazelton, p. 43.

French soldiers. They are merely braver five minutes longer."

What effects have you experienced from enduring adversity?

Military people say the test of a good army is how well it fights when it is tired. Likewise, the strength of personal character is displayed by a person who keeps going when the way is rough, who keeps fighting when weary. Strength is increased through exerting extra effort when you have about reached your limit.

Christian maturity is a goal to be pursued.

Christian maturity is not attained through one grand leap of faith, or one climactic emotional experience, but through persistent effort. It is a goal to be pursued rather than a state to be attained. The perfect and complete person is the transcendent goal that keeps us from settling down into self-righteousness and complacency. Endurance and steadfastness is the key to such maturity, according to James.

Conversion is the decision which initiates a process.

The Beatitudes and other teachings of Jesus lift up this goal of becoming a complete, or perfect, person through continued effort. The New Testament defines conversion as the decision which initiates a process. That process is the means for attaining Christian maturity.

I have just listened to a tape recording of a lady practicing speech therapy. A stroke left her with the loss of the power of speech. In order to speak she must now develop a different part of the brain to carry on this function.

It is no small matter to have a function you have known for 60 years taken away. Unusual effort is required to meet such a test.

Self-pity would be an easy pitfall for this lady. However, she has faced this adversity with courage and determination. Along with her household chores, she spends part of each day forming simple words, learning thought patterns and retraining herself to speak.

The stroke was certainly not a blessing, but she had some great experiences of friendship and love, some new challenges, in the midst of this trial and adversity. What could have been a total defeat was accepted as a challenge and met with joyful anticipation of living.

Steadfast faith is confident trust.

I have seen a courage and steadfast faith in this lady that has been inspiring. Growth in adversity is a wealth that cannot be obtained with the gold and silver of this world. It is a heavenly wealth. It indicates a wealth of character and maturity.

I have a friend who has experienced an unusual amount of sorrow and suffering. Her thirteen-year-old-son was killed on a hunting trip. Soon afterward her father suffered a heart attack and died. A few months later her mother died after spending months in the hospital with a lingering disease.

In addition to all this sorrow, there were other difficulties and trials. Bitterness and cynicism would have been an easy response to the pain and agony of these adversities. Yet, she endured. She kept a positive attitude toward life, remained steadfast in her faith and met the requirements of each day.

In the midst of this suffering she made a significant achievement in her professional career. It is not easy to maintain the discipline of a profession, deal with the needs of others and undergo testing when your heart is breaking and you are burdened down with trouble.

She demonstrated in her life what James is calling for in all Christian disciples. Such endurance and positive response is the key to the victory of life.

Endurance and a positive response to adversity is the key to a victorious life.

The unspoken witness of her capacity to endure without retreating into self-pity and without giving up is an effective witness. This lady is a living witness to the victory that comes through endurance, discipline, and positive response.

Joy for many persons comes in the strength to live through adversity. The "crown of life" about which James writes comes to those who endure trial, meet the tests and remain steadfast. While James doesn't define that "crown," the New Testament defines it as the garland of victory of the athlete. After the contest the award is given to the winner. The faithful and steadfast Christian disciples are the true winners in life.

Finding meaning and beauty in the hidden and difficult places means the Christian has a deeper sense of joy and happiness. The truly joyful person is one who finds good even when circumstances are hard and life is tough.

While our Lord "never promised you a rose garden," he does promise his peace and joy.

Perhaps Dostoevski perceived a secret many of us miss. He wrote, "There is only one thing that I dread: not to be worthy of my sufferings." May God make us worthy of our sufferings. Herein is strength, character and joy.

Viktor Frankl, the psychiatrist who developed such keen insights and deep understandings of man during his World War II imprisonment by the Nazis, has written, "What man actually needs is not a tensionless state but rather the striving and struggling for some goal worthy of him." [2] This is precisely what James is saying to us. "Count it all joy, my brethren, when you meet various trials, for you know that the testing of your faith produces steadfastness." (1:2-3).

(1:2-3)
Count it all joy, my brethren, when you meet various trials, for you know that the testing of your faith produces steadfastness.

[2] *Man's Search For Meaning,* p. 166.

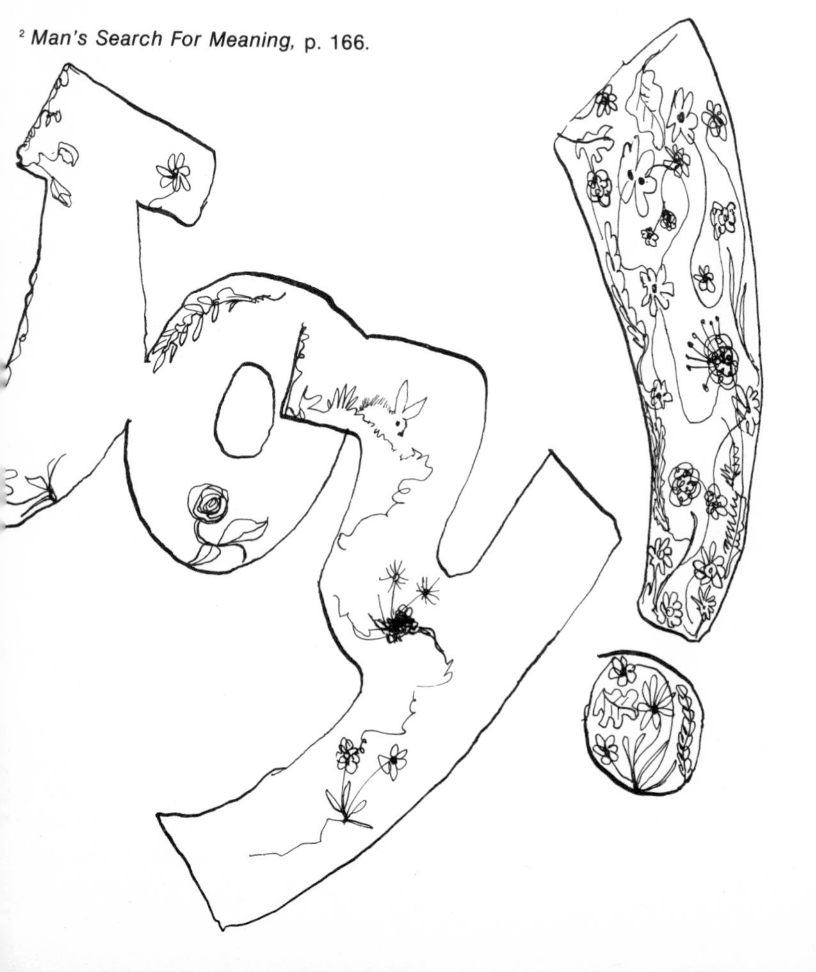

integrity!

chapter 2

Games People Play

A popular song has made us painfully aware of the pitfall of insincerity. With a "mod" beat to the music, the lyrics speak of the insincere person who misuses religious faith.

"Oh the games people play now
Every night and every day now
Never meaning what they
say now
Never saying what they mean.

This is indeed a sad commentary on the dishonesty that creeps into the lives of people. There are those in our society who just play games. They never back up their pious talk with actions consistent with what they say. For them, religion is kept in one compartment and never relates to the rest of life. Their actions toward others are never seen as the real expression of religion.

There is something in all of us that abhors phoniness. Yet, we are all guilty of pretense and phoniness at times. The price of authenticity and genuineness is constant vigilance and sincere examination of motives.

(1:19-27)

Know this, my beloved brethren. Let every man be quick to hear, slow to speak, slow to anger, for the anger of man does not work the righteousness of God. Therefore put away all filthiness and rank growth of wickedness and receive with meekness the implanted word, which is able to save your souls.

But be doers of the word, and not hearers only, deceiving yourselves. For if any one is a hearer of the word and not a doer, he is like a man who observes his natural face in a mirror; for he observes himself and goes away and at once forgets what he was like. But he who looks into the perfect law, the law of liberty, and perseveres, being no hearer that forgets but a doer that acts, he shall be blessed in his doing.

If any one thinks he is religious, and does not bridle his tongue but deceives his heart, this man's religion is vain. Religion that is pure and undefiled before God and the Father is this: to visit orphans and widows in their affliction, and to keep oneself unstained from the world.

Genuine religion is marked by two characteristics: practical kindness and personal purity. These are the primary characteristics that make religion acceptable with God. These elements produce genuineness and sincerity and rid the life of phoniness.

Both Jesus and the Old Testament prophets make clear the importance of exercising responsible care for those in need. James specifies those in need as widows and orphans, but he does not mean to exclude others who need help. They simply illustrate the concern for persons in need that should characterize the disciple of Christ.

Practicing justice and charity in one's own life and insisting on the same in the larger society is the natural outgrowth of the Word being implanted in one's heart. Long ago Micah (6:8) defined the genuine religious life: "He showed you, O man, what is good; and what does the Lord require of you but to do justice, and to love kindness, and to walk humbly with your God?"

There are certain things that are incompatible with our life as Christian disciples. Some of the alien elements described by James are: "man's anger cannot promote the justice (righteousness) of God" and "away then with all that is sordid." James does not exhaust the things which might be incompatible with our discipleship. However the list is suggestive, allowing the reader to define for himself other alien elements. This is another example of James' practical method of instructing new converts.

James doesn't merely give vague, general instructions about purity of life and conduct. He states specifically the things that make a life impure and indicate phoniness.

A wild and unruly tongue indicates an imperfect or immature personality. Learning the discipline of self-control is basic to developing a sincere, genuine inner life.

James deals rather strongly with the tongue. While some may think he has overstated the case, no one can deny that the tongue can be devastating in its treatment of persons. It can also be a significant means of expressing kindness and goodness.

Keeping oneself unspotted from the world means to avoid clinging to the affections, fashions, values, and pleasures of this society which ignores the divine Father. The Christian disciple is to remember that his values are more permanent, his pleasure more lasting, and his hope more certain than that which a transitory society can offer.

Write a paraphrase of 1:27.

The genuinely religious person isn't "playing games" but seeking to be honest and true. An ability to perform certain outward rituals is not enough. There must be single and sincere devotion to God demonstrated by compassionate regard for others, there must be life lived in harmony with the purposes of the will of God.

Self-deceit is a dangerous game. It can produce such distortions that it is difficult to recover a true self-image and accurate understanding. Living a half-truth or lie is a poor way to live.

What we need to do is take off our masks and be our real selves. Pretense is all right for the stage but it won't work in real life. Phony living produces phony people (or is it vice versa?) and there is no possibility of satisfying life when it's based on phoniness. Be honest. Be authentic. Be consistent. Thus, you can be a true person and real.

James gives hard-hitting advice regarding phony religion, fooling yourself. Read those passages and reflect on your own life. Determine now that you will permit the grace of God to take such root in your life that you will be a real person, not a phony.

Recently, I spent a day at a Roman Catholic Monastery with some friends. We had purposed to get apart, take off the masks and get to know our real selves. For most of us it was easy to sit in small groups and say, "I think thus and so," but it was painfully difficult to say, "I feel this way."

Most of us cultivate the art of hiding our real selves. We need to cultivate the art of being our real selves. We need to develop the ability to share our true selves. Only then can we be authentically religious persons.

Only those who break out of the prison of isolation and self-centeredness, see the needs of others, and respond in love and compassion are real persons.

Make a list of the inconsistencies most commonly found in the lives of people today.

chapter 3

Closing The Gap Between How You Talk And How You Walk

James 2:14 is the famous indictment of a faith that doesn't act. James contends that genuine faith produces works. He makes it clear that just because you talk about faith is no sign you have faith. There must be evidence of your faith.

Here is where many have erred. We have mistaken pious talk, or faith language, for the fact. True faith isn't a set of words or language. It is a living relationship in which the believer is empowered and enabled to live the Christ-like life.

It is erroneous to think that holding certain beliefs is adequate. Belief becomes faith only when it produces action. The writer points out that "even the demons believe and shudder." Such belief is only an idea in the brain. Faith is an understanding energized by commitment of will that accepts responsibility. Faith is the dynamic that sets in motion good-will, righteousness and concern.

(2:14-26)
What does it profit, my brethren, if a man says he has faith but has not works? Can his faith save him? If a brother or sister is ill-clad and in lack of daily food, and one of you say to them, "Go in peace, be warmed and filled," without giving them the things needed for the body, what does it profit? So faith by itself, if it has not works, is dead.
But some one will say, "You have faith and I have works." Show me your faith apart from your works, and I by my works will show you my faith. You believe that God is one; you do well. Even the demons believe and shudder. Do you want to be shown, you foolish fellow, that faith apart from works is barren? Was not Abraham our father justified

by works, when he offered his son Isaac upon the altar? You see that faith was active along with his works, and faith was completed by works, and the scripture was fulfilled which says, "Abraham believed God, and it was reckoned to him as righteousness"; and he was called the friend of God. You see that a man is justified by works and not by faith alone. And in the same way was not also Rahab the harlot justified by works when she received the messengers and sent them out another way? For as the body apart from the spirit is dead, so faith apart from works is dead.

Perhaps the most effective argument James uses is the simple statement: "For as the body apart from the Spirit is dead, so faith apart from the works is dead." The energy of works keeps faith alive, vital.

The gospel is not a set of beliefs to be stored in the mind, nor is it a good feeling to be held in the heart. It is a message to be shared, a life to be given, a reconciliation to be effected. Jesus came not to be served but to serve and give his life for others. Likewise, our relationship with God is not something to exult in, but a call to obey, a mission to fulfill. It is a personal ministry to carry out rather than a statement of beliefs.

When we witness to God's redeeming love in words, we must demonstrate it in deeds. Our walk must be consistent with our talk. Consistency of belief and action constitutes true faith.

Merely expressing pious good wishes must not be mistaken for faith. To repeat a creed without living up to it is as grotesquely futile as to feed the starving with unctuous good wishes. Dr. Albert E. Barnett used to say to his class in New Testament at Emory University, "Faith is not a substitute for goodness; it is an energy for the achievement of goodness."

Toyohiko Kagawa, the Japanese Christian who made such a lasting impact on his nation pointed out to his people: "It is not enough to have ideals. We must translate them into action. We must clear our own little corner of creation." In a meditative poem he makes specific this statement.

Draw up two columns. In one put down the things you profess to stand for, to believe. In the other, put down the things you actually practice.

Holding a beggar's child
against my heart,
Through blinding tears I see
That as I love the tiny, piteous thing,
So God loves me!

Kagawa closed the gap between what he said and what he did. Faith resulted in deed. This is the true life described in the New Testament.

In too many instances personal salvation has been allowed to be a stagnant pool. Elton Trueblood says: "It would be hard to defend the worth of faith, for example, in which people rejoice in their own personal salvation while they pay little or no attention to the economic and racial injustices about them." He goes on to warn of the danger of humanism: "But it is equally tragic to witness what is really the greater danger at this period of our history, the development of social action divorced

What are the elements in authentic healthy religion?

Faith empowers persons and groups to do God's will, shoulder the burdens of others and walk in love.

from any cultivation of either reverence or humility."[1]

James doesn't suggest we do not need faith. The social conscience needs to be nurtured in a deep personal experience of God's love. Ethical actions are to flow out of the experience of God's righteous love. Faith empowers persons and groups to do God's will, shoulder the burdens of others and walk in love.

Karl Barth speaks forcefully to the true Christian life: "May every individual Christian be clear that so long as his faith is a snail's shell in which he feels comfortable, but which does not bother itself with the life of his people, so long, that is, as he lives in dualism, he has not yet really come to believe! This snail's shell is not a desirable residence. It is not good to be here. Man is a whole and can only exist as such a whole."[2]

When there is a separation of talk from walk, man is split and divided. The New Testament knows no dichotomy between faith and deed. The inner life expresses itself in outer deeds. A piety that is exclusively devotional or intellectual is counterfeit. Consistency of belief and action constitutes true faith. Such true faith is our goal in religious nurture and experience.

[1] *The Future of the Christian* by Elton Trueblood, p. 11.
[2] *Dogmatics in Outline* by Karl Barth, p. 34.

chapter 4

Being Wise Is More Than Being Educated

(1:5-11)
If any of you lacks wisdom, let him ask God who gives to all men generously and without reproaching, and it will be given him. But let him ask in faith, with no doubting, for he who doubts is like a wave of the sea that is driven and tossed by the wind. For that person must not suppose that a double-minded man, unstable in all his ways, will receive anything from the Lord. Let the lowly brother boast in his exaltation, and the rich in his humiliation, because like the flower of the grass he will pass away. For the sun rises with its scorching heat and withers the grass; its flower falls, and its beauty perishes. So will the rich man fade away in the midst of his pursuits.

Our society puts a high price on knowledge. Education has a high priority in western culture. In fact, public education has been credited by many persons with making democracy work as well as it has in the United States. From infancy on we feel compelled to impart knowledge to people and train them.

In the past 50 years there has been a knowledge explosion, its size unprecedented in the entire history of mankind. For example, there are more scientists living today than in all the rest of human history all together. This knowledge explosion has left us with more educated people in the western world, than have ever existed.

However, there is ample evidence which indicates that with all our mental sharpness, our vast knowledge, we aren't really wise. You can be intelligent and have much knowledge, but if you can't relate this knowledge to daily life

(3:13-18)
Who is wise and understanding among you? By his good life let him show his works in the meekness of wisdom. But if you have bitter jealousy and selfish ambition in your hearts, do not boast and be false to the truth. This wisdom is not such as comes down from above, but is earthly, unspiritual, devilish. For where jealousy and selfish ambition exist, there will be disorder and every vile practice. But the wisdom from above is first pure, then peaceable, gentle, open to reason, full of mercy and good fruits, without uncertainty or insincerity. And the harvest of righteousness is sown in peace by those who make peace.

Now, what is wisdom?

How can we get wisdom from God?

Is a high IQ a guarantee of a good life?

in a meaningful way you can still be a stupid person.

There are a great many educated, learned people who do not possess wisdom. They know many facts but do not know the proper application of those facts for the greatest benefit of mankind.

It is at this point that we are in trouble in our society. Our grasp of knowledge has exceeded our ability to apply and utilize that knowledge to produce a good life. It is not enough to know how to split atoms, we must be wise enough to put atomic energy to good use. Our technological knowledge now threatens to undo us. Our earth is being polluted beyond livability. We are producing so much throw-away material, we may bury ourselves under our own trash.

Thus, James urges his readers to seek wisdom from God. He assures them that God will give wisdom to the sincere, single-minded person. In the second portion where he deals with wisdom, he describes the difference between wisdom and knowledge.

A good mind is a gift from God. Like other gifts from God, we ought to use it wisely. Having the gift of a good mind is one thing, knowing how to use it is another matter. True wisdom is also a gift from God. Like faith it is manifest in good patterns of life, in good works, and in such virtues as meekness and humility.

Use newspaper clippings to show how our vast knowledge does not necessarily equip us to deal with real life.

One Bible scholar has reminded us that "Wisdom for Israel was more than intellectual knowledge; it meant that grasp of reality which enabled a man rightly to discern the issues of life and rightly to conduct his life by that insight."[1] For the Hebrew, true wisdom was rooted in a right attitude to God. (Note Proverbs 9:10; 15:33; Psalm 111:10).

In our own day we are called to the task of leading people to the true source of wisdom. (Ephesians 1:17; Acts 7:10). The question confronting us is: Who will capture the minds and wills of this generation? When we allow film makers, producers of paperback novels and television directors to decide the thinking and acting of people, we do so at our own risk. The violence and chaos that is threatening the fabric of our society is the result of allowing the wrong forces to shape the thinking and condition the climate.

(Ephesians 1:17)
That the God of our Lord Jesus Christ, the Father of glory, may give you a spirit of wisdom and of revelation in the knowledge of him.
(Acts 7:10)
And rescued him out of all his afflictions, and gave him favor and wisdom before Pharaoh, king of Egypt, who made him governor over Egypt and over all his household.

With the decline of church schools and other traditional opportunities for study, small groups take on added importance. It is

[1] *Torch Bible Paperbacks* by A. S. Herbert, p. 129.

absolutely imperative for us to help people get wisdom and understanding. Only as they are free and honest, sincere and searching can it happen.

Do we have a responsibility to help people study and discover truth?

People are ill-equipped to meet the complexities of this day. Sharp ethical questions loom up before us which we have not previously had to answer. Traditional concepts do not readily apply to the situations we face today. As James says, we must ask God for new wisdom.

Christians are called to outthink non-Christians in order to apply the knowledge of God in creative and beneficial ways to the questions and problems of men.

True wisdom is marked by a search for truth.

Half-truths and partial facts quite often lead to faulty decisions. It is too dangerous to fool around with partial truth today. The stakes are too great! A genuine desire for wisdom rather than knowledge would help us avoid a lot of errors and point us to a wholesome life.

Solomon is the biblical figure best known for his wisdom. When God offered to grant him any wish he desired, Solomon asked for wisdom and knowledge so that he would be able to rule over the great nation of Israel. Riches, honor, power, long life were side benefits but they came because he prized wisdom for the right reason. Much later he wrote, "Wisdom is better than rubies; and all the things that may be desired are not to be compared to it" (Proverbs 8:11).

Before you leave these portions of James notice how he defines wisdom. It is pure, peaceable, gentle, open to reason, full of mercy, without uncertainty, without insincerity, and without hypocrisy. No wonder he considers the wise as the only happy people. Therefore, let us ask for the wisdom God gives.

WAR
selfish
strife
hate

chapter 5

Who Started The Hatfield-McCoy Feud?

Today's newspaper described one conflict after another. There were stories of international war, national conflict, murder, strife between individuals and all of these described men's inability to get along with each other.

Feuding and fussing are the continuing result of the inner strife in mankind. Who started the Hatfield-McCoy feud? Whoever expressed a haughty, jealous spirit which disregarded the rights and needs of others is responsible for the climate of feuding.

Get a copy of the famous prayer by St. Francis of Assisi: "Lord, make me an instrument of Thy Peace." Commit it to memory.

Selfishness, according to James, is the root problem. Conflict and strife are born out of our selfish desires which fail to regard the needs and interests of others.

Wrangling and bickering are the result of uncontrolled desires and passions which seem to find no satisfaction. Such unbridled passion and selfishness can harm others and even lead to murder.

Peace is the result of inner control and order. The soul that is submitted to God in faithfulness and loyalty is equipped to meet temptations and remain steadfast.

James warns them that God will not be satisfied with divided allegiance. He calls them "unfaithful creatures," or "adulteresses." You can't be faithful to two loves at one time. Either give yourself to complete devotion to God or to the world. It is impossible to hold to both.

When communities are faithful to the finest and noblest, the righteous, there is peace. Quarrelling and fighting are absent when members of a community or nation have learned the meaning of compassion. It is selfish acquisitiveness, whether under the guise of communism or imperialism, that produces conflict, war, and hostility.

Peace for the individual is likewise found in the giving up of self and learning submission to God.

Short fuses and bad explosions can be avoided by learning love, patience and concern for others. The pressure many of us are under that produces bad tempers is the result of unwarranted ambitions and inordinate desires.

When we begin to feel the worth of each person, we see our own lives in a truer perspective. In this way we learn to be impartial, refusing to play favorites or accept the social standards of the world. Have you noticed how prone we all are to name-dropping, social climbing or partiality to persons who meet standards set by the world? Such partiality and snobbishness are referred to in 2:1-7 and condemned as contrary to the spirit of Jesus. Partiality based on outward appearance is the beginning of hostility between persons. Avoiding partiality is a means to good relations.

James' emphasis on the tongue cannot be overlooked in this matter of people living in harmony. He describes it as a "fire." He goes on to say "with it we bless the Lord and Father, and with it we curse men, who are made in the likeness of God" (3:9). It is our primary means of communication.

No person ever built friendship, peace and harmony with an unruly tongue. Careless words can hurt reputation, break up friendship, leave scars that are hard to heal. James makes it clear that the Christian disciple must learn to control the tongue.

Self-control is the mark of the mature person. Short fuses cause bad explosions and these are the result of an immature person. If

(2:1-7)

My brethren, show no partiality as you hold the faith of our Lord Jesus Christ, the Lord of glory. For if a man with gold rings and in fine clothing comes into your assembly, and a poor man in shabby clothing also comes in, and you pay attention to the one who wears the fine clothing and say, "Have a seat here, please," while you say to the poor man, "Stand there," or "Sit at my feet, have you not made distinctions among yourselves, and become judges with evil thoughts? Listen, my beloved brethren. Has not God chosen those who are poor in the world to be rich in faith and heirs of the kingdom which he has promised to those who love him? But you have dishonored the poor man. Is it not the rich who oppress you, is it not they who drag you into court? Is it not they who blaspheme that honorable name by which you are called?

we look closely enough we will find that it all roots back to childish insistence on having our own way. The domineering, dogmatic person has failed to learn how to work with and get along with other people. James has plenty to say about these matters. Perhaps this is why we are so uncomfortable reading his words.

James deals with three basic problems in human relationships: hostility that leads to conflict; partiality and snobbishness that subvert the real worth of persons; the uncontrolled use of the tongue. These are not related to one day and age but to all time and people.

What practical steps for peace can you take? How about learning about other nations, other races so you can appreciate their history, needs, dreams.

Today, we are wrestling with the threat of international holocaust unless we find the means of settling differences without conflict. To work for peace is not a nice hobby for a few but the demand of the gospel for all of us. We are called to be "Peacemakers" in the world threatened by hostility and conflict, hate and misunderstanding.

Violence and crime are now reaching epidemic proportions. Social scientists and psychologists are working hard to find the causes and cures. It may be that our hope lies in the simple return to teaching kindness rather than anger, sharing rather than selfish acquisition.

A return to law and order will not be achieved simply by tougher laws and more arrests. There must be a new attitude of respect for human personality, a determination to insure the rights of others.

We must promote a new set of heroes, other than the swashbuckling gangster or tough, fast-shooting cowboy. Perhaps we should take a second-look at the "flower children," peaceniks" etc. If they can help us overcome the image of the strong person as violent-oriented they will have made a valuable contribution.

However, peace is more than the absence of physical violence. It is a genuine regard for justice, human dignity and opportunity. Oppression is also a form of violence and can be just as deadly.

(Matthew 6:19)
Do not lay up for yourselves treasures on earth, where moth and rust consume and where thieves break in and steal.

chapter 6

Counting On The Future

James begins this chapter by continuing to warn his readers about overemphasis on wealth. Allowing themselves to put their hope in riches that deteriorate has caused them to abuse their fellow man in order to obtain luxury and pleasure. It has also diminished their confidence in the future. Notice the similarity of these passages to the words of Jesus in Matthew 6:19.

The wealthy are condemned for two errors: first, they place too much hope in possessions and find their satisfactions in luxury; second, they fail to act responsibly toward the poor.

Possessing wealth isn't condemned. Attachment to material wealth is the mistake James warns his readers about. In these passages there is the underlying conviction that the material world is not permanent.

Their failure to practice justice and share abundance with the poor and destitute is severely condemned. His instructions are

(5:1-12)
Come now, you rich, weep and howl for the miseries that are coming upon you. Your riches have rotted and your garments are motheaten. Your gold and silver have rusted, and their rust will be evidence against you and will eat your flesh like fire. You have laid up treasure for the last days.
Behold, the wages of the laborers who mowed your fields, which you kept back by fraud, cry out; and the cries of the harvesters have reached the ears of the Lord of hosts. You have lived on the earth in luxury and in pleasure; you have fattened your hearts in a day of slaughter. You have condemned, you have killed the righteous man; he does not resist you.
Be patient, therefore, brethren, until the coming of the Lord.

Behold, the farmer waits for the precious fruit of the earth, being patient over it until it receives the early and the late rain. You also be patient. Establish your hearts, for the coming of the Lord is at hand.

Do not grumble, brethren, against one another, that you may not be judged; behold, the Judge is standing at the doors. As an example of suffering and patience, brethren, take the prophets who spoke in the name of the Lord. Behold, we call those happy who were steadfast. You have heard of the steadfastness of Job, and you have seen the purpose of the Lord, how the Lord is compassionate and merciful.

But above all, my brethren, do not swear, either by heaven or by earth or with any other oath, but let your yes be yes and your no be no, that you may not fall under condemnation.

clear and forthright on the matter.

In 5:7 James touches on the controversial second coming of Christ. The phrase "coming of the Lord" or "coming of the Lord Jesus Christ" is frequently referred to in the Gospels and the writings of Paul.

Unfortunately, this idea has been grossly misinterpreted and has produced a sense of fear or dread in many people. It was not intended to do so originally. For those early disciples it indicated a certain hope.

True enough, some followers in the early church misunderstood it to mean an immediate apocalyptic event. The author of 2 Peter points out that their sense of timing is not in harmony with God's timescale: "Here is one point, my friends, which you must not lose sight of: With the Lord one day is like a thousand years and a thousand years like one day." (3:8)

Christians are to live as though the rule of God in Christ is an immediate possibility. It gives a focus to life and makes hope substantive.

The Lord is constantly coming in our world to assert his rule and to redeem life. However, there will come a time, when no man knows, when his rule will come to full fruition. This will be the grand finale of the divine human drama. The scripture writers spoke of this as the "end of time." By this, is not meant the destruction of time or the world but the completion of God's will and purpose.

Do you have a sense of urgency in your Christian discipleship? Those who anticipate Christ live with a sense of urgency to minister, to reconcile, to witness.

There isn't any reason to believe that God intends to destroy his world or end the human race. His presence will finally be known and adored in a full and complete way. By the "end" scripture writers mean the time of summing up or bringing to completion.

James urges his readers to be patient in their anticipation of Christ. They are to live with a sense of trust in the redemptive purpose of God to work its way in human history.

Discouragement in the face of injustice and oppression is the constant pitfall for the disciple of Jesus. Like ourselves those early Christians were tempted to be disheartened because of the delay of the vindication of right and the ultimate triumph of our Lord.

In spite of this we are to remain constant in our loyalty and devotion. Our hope is not based on outward appearance and that which is seen. Our hope remains in the certainty of Christ's triumph. The long interval between the promise of triumph and accom-

plishment is the time for steadfast loyalty and patient anticipation.

Without hope life is a dismal experience. Those who find hope only in this temporal world must be quite frantic. Real hope is available for those who anticipate God's continuing deliverance in the coming of Christ.

Anticipating Christ as the answer to the human dilemma is the means by which life is stabilized. Looking forward to the presence of Christ gives a quality to living in the present moment.

In these passages there is the underlying conviction that the material world is not permanent. He reminds them, "You have piled up wealth in an age that is near its close." (v. 3).

The writer urges them to exercise patience in waiting for the coming of the Lord. The apparent delay of the expected arrival of the Lord had caused them to be impatient and had produced misunderstandings.

For some the idea of a second coming of Christ is frightening. Others see it as an escape hatch out of the problems of life. But James wanted them to have a different mind.

Today we are to anticipate Christ as the daily deliverer. He arrives in many ways to redeem us and reassert his rule in human society. Our sense of anticipation ought to include the expectation of a day when he brings to completion his redemption of life.

This hope allows us to count on the future. In fact, "Christ in you, the hope of glory" is the New Testament secret for confidence.

More than just waiting for the future, though, it is the reason for a determined effort to create the society where Christ is loved and served. This hope produces impetus not apathy.

It is easy to get discouraged with the mighty forces of evil and the secular society in such visible presence. The word needs to be spoken to us that the victory of God is sure and Christ's triumph is certain. Therefore, renew your obedience and remain steadfast against the forces of evil. Count on the future as you anticipate the fulness of the coming of Christ.

chapter 7

Life's Biggest Challenge

These passages resume the theme of 1:9-11 and 2:1-7 in dealing with judgment on the rich. Evidently James considered it important enough for repetition.

Condemnation is rendered on the wealthy who have obtained their wealth by oppressing the poor. Exploiting people for personal gain is opposed to the spirit of Christ who was the servant of men. There is no basis for believing that a man can be in right relationship with God if he is acting unjustly toward his fellow man.

From Amos to Jesus there are strong words for those who substitute pious talk for responsible action for others. Our faith has a great deal to do with how we obtain and spend our money. Stewardship is more than just giving to the church; it also has to do with how we obtain our resources.

If James were writing today I suspect he would also deal with those who exploit the natural resources and short-change unborn generations. The righteous man has to consider how he uses this

(5:1-6)
Come now, you rich, weep and howl for the miseries that are coming upon you. Your riches have rotted and your garments are motheaten. Your gold and silver have rusted, and their rust will be evidence against you and will eat your flesh like fire. You have laid up treasure for the last days. Behold, the wages of the laborers who mowed your fields, which you kept back by fraud, cry out; and the cries of the harvesters have reached the ears of the Lord of hosts. You have lived on the earth in luxury and in pleasure; you have fattened your hearts in a day of slaughter. You have condemned, you have killed the righteous man; he does not resist you.

Make a collage depicting the values of our society.

world God has given to us. He can rape the good earth, but this doesn't harmonize with his profession of love for God. If we love God, we will evidence loving care for his world and his children.

Extravagance and luxury are out of character for the person who serves God. Such a person evidences compassionate concern for the common welfare of human society. Colin Morris puts it to us with sharpness in his book. He says, "We pursue our private obsessions whilst mankind is laid waste about us. Only the well-fed play at church. The rest are too busy raking dust bins and garbage heaps for a morsel to feed their children.[1]

Love of Christ drives out greed and selfishness. Luxurious living is absurd for the follower of him who was of such simple tastes.

Luxury and pleasure are the means by which the rich prepare their own doom. Basing their lives on these false values, they are left with values that decay and are worthless but the means by which they were obtained and the regard with which they were held rise up to haunt them.

In every age Christians need to re-think sense of values. Constant

Clip from magazines and newspapers pictures and stories that describe true values. Share these with members of your group or other friends.

[1] *Include Me Out* by Colin Morris, p. 58.

vigilance over the human spirit to prevent selfish exploitation and inordinate affection for the transitory is imperative for the man of faith.

To escape the miseries of disappointment and emptiness we must search for the real. You don't have to go very far to find the real. Amazingly enough real values can be found in your own family and with your neighbors. You don't have to enter into austere circumstances to discover true values. Considering the deeper needs of others is the beginning of appropriating lasting values.

Tell your family what they mean to you.
Write a note to a friend expressing appreciation to him for his friendship.

Riches and social status are insecure foundations for life. The prestige and wealth that men count important are bursting bubbles, at best, and, at worst, the source of disappointment and despair. Samuel Shoemaker has pointed out that "the surest symbol of a heart not yet fully subdued to God and his will is going to be found in the areas of money, sex and power; in wanting these things for ourselves."[2] He goes on to say, "surest symbol of spiritual earnestness will be the checkbook, the affections, and the ego drive surrendered to him." It must be clearly understood that

[2] *The Experiment of Faith* by Samuel Shoemaker, p. 37.

the denial or repression of these things is not the objective. The secret lies in the surrender of these things to God so that human personality may be fulfilled and the noblest purposes served.

Life's biggest challenge is learning to surrender the basic drives and the simplest pleasures, the desires and impulses to God. Thus, wealth can be godly rather than godless exploitation of others and indication of selfishness.

chapter 8

The Court Of First Resort

These closing paragraphs contain characteristic notes from the previous chapters. The value of prayer has been the insistent plea of James. Here he puts it in terms of prayer for the sick. In adversity prayer is the first resort.

Here the writer describes the availability of God and the ministry we have to each other.

In all the circumstances of life we are to turn to God. In suffering Christians are to pray. In experiences of joy they are to sing praises.

A person who is sick should call for elders of the church to pray and anoint with oil. The presence of the church leaders symbolizes a circle of love and a caring community. The value of people who care cannot be overestimated.

Loneliness and rejection are devastating to human personality. In the same way love and acceptance exert powerful healing on persons.

Oil symbolizes the healing powers of God. Those early

(5:13-20)
Is any one among you suffering? Let him pray. Is any cheerful? Let him sing praise. Is any among you sick? Let him call for the elders of the church, and let them pray over him, anointing him with oil in the name of the Lord; and the prayer of faith will save the sick man, and the Lord will raise him up; and if he has committed sins, he will be forgiven. Therefore confess your sins to one another, and pray for one another, that you may be healed. The prayer of a righteous man has great power in its effects. Elijah was a man of like nature with ourselves and he prayed fervently that it might not rain, and for three years and six months it did not rain on the earth. Then he prayed again and the heaven gave rain, and the earth brought forth its fruit.

My brethren, if any one among you wanders from the truth and some one brings him back, let him know that whoever brings back a sinner from the error of his way will save his soul from death and will cover a multitude of sins.

Make a list of the problems you have with prayer. Be honest.

Learn to pray short prayers of adoration, confession, thanksgiving and for others.

church leaders did not understand the oil to have any magical medicinal property. It just symbolized a sacramental effect.

So-called "faith-healing" has been abused, distorted, and mismanaged. Some persons outright reject it while others make too broad claims. Leslie Weatherhead has given us keen insight in his classic work *Psychology, Religion and Healing.*

The primary point is that God desires the health and well-being of the whole man, body and soul. Death and disease also have a place in God's ordering of things. However, through the ages the church has followed Jesus in praying hopefully and faithfully for physical health and spiritual restoration.

The forgiveness of sin, getting rid of the load of guilt is closely tied to health and well-being. This alliance is not accidental.

Honest confession is the beginning of wholeness and healing. Secret sins, buried resentments, latent hostilities are some of the malignant forces that eat away inner health and well-being.

Prayer, James reiterates throughout his book, is the answer to all the needs of your life. There is power in prayer. It energizes the forces in one's life. When prayer is backed up by a good life it is truly powerful and effective.

Prayer, according to James, is not a complicated theory but a simple act of expressing feelings to the Father. Rosalind Rinker has captured the spirit of the New Testament concept of prayer in her practice of conversational prayer. She has stripped it of the outer layers and put it in simple, personal terms of expressing genuine feelings.

The closing verses of the book deal in a specific way with the personal ministry of Christian disciples. It ends on a note of hope for those who go astray and promise of reward for those who turn the erring brother.

James clearly sees the role of every Christian as having a ministry to perform. In the early church there wasn't the division between clergy and laity. Every disciple shared in the responsibility of witnessing to the gospel and serving the needs of his fellow man.

When the church has been most like its Lord there has been a compassionate concern for the hopeless people of society. The church in its best moments has seen possibilities of redemption in the most desperate cases.

Make a list of the powerless people who need your ministry.

Our function is to reach out to

redeem, not to reject and condemn. Society condemns and punishes but the Christian community reconciles and redeems.

Is it enough to give money?

What a magnificent calling for us in this day and time! There is so much brokenness and need all about us and we are the reconciling agents of God. Each of us has a personal ministry. We are enjoined to find the erring brothers and guide them into the light of the truth.

Small groups are playing a major role in helping persons and groups find their ministry. Many persons have found healing and wholeness through sharing, study, and prayer. But, they are discovering more than personal wholeness. These groups have enabled persons to get into mission.

Listen to some of Johnny Cash's music on missions—see if this doesn't make you more aware and sensitive to the needs of others.

A small group of youth in a small southern town caught a vision of ministry to prisoners. Each week they visited the local jail and read to inmates, talked with them and let them know someone cared. They also went to a nearby state prison and conducted worship. The warden told the group's pastor that a few weeks after the group started, there was a significant change in the atmosphere and morale in the prison.

There are opportunities in every city or community for reaching out to forgotten, lonely and lost people. As the song says, "What the world needs now is love." There is healing and wholeness in love and acceptance. We can bring God's healing to others through our ministry of love and acceptance. This is our calling. God help us to hear and heed.

Who are the lost, lonely, forgotten?

Bruce Larson and Ralph Osborne urge churches as well as individuals to dream dreams and catch visions. They write: "God is in the dream business for the church at large and for local congregations as much as for any individual or group. Every local church needs to discover that it has a general and a particular ministry entrusted to it at any given time. This will be contingent upon the opportunities and problems that surround it, and the wider cultural situation in which it finds itself." [1]

Surely God is calling churches and persons to move out of their comfortable havens and minister to the real needs of real people. Churches as well as individuals or small groups can become self-centered and introspective rather than involved with the hurt of people.

Prayer is a power source.

James instructs us to pray and then to reach out to people in need. Prayer is not a last resort

[1] *The Emerging Church* by Bruce Larson and Ralph Osborne, pp. 146-7.

when all else has failed. Prayer is the first resource where power is needed to minister to others. This is the name of the game: personal ministry.

notes

notes

notes

my strategies for doing my faith